Change My Story
OH LORD

Powerful prayers and scriptures to change your destiny

Call unto me and I shall answer thee and show thee great and mighty things which you know not - Jeremiah 33:3 (NIV)

Bishop Dickson Juma Omukosi

Change My Story OH LORD © *2023*
Bishop Dickson Juma Omukosi

All rights reserved.

No part of this publication may be reproduced, distributed, or transmitted in any form or by any means, including photocopying, recording, or other electronic or mechanical methods, without the prior written permission of the publisher, except in the case of brief quotations embodied in critical reviews and certain other noncommercial uses permitted by copyright law.

Contents

Dedication iii

Acknowledgments iv

About v

Bishop Dickson Juma Omukosi v

Introduction vii

Preface ix

Called To Pray 1

Command Your Day 9

Restoration Prayers 19

Prayer Petitions 29

Family And Self Deliverance 39

Breaking The Chains Of Stagnation 51

Spirit Of Delay 63

Breaking The Curse Of Poverty 75

Spiritual Warfare 83

Dedication

This book is dedicated to the Royal Family of Matayo Khisa for encouraging me to go for the best; the blessed Omukosi Family for the humble time given to me to write this book and to the Zion Family for prayers and support. God bless you all.

Acknowledgments

Special thanks to the team at D.F. Publishing and Church Girl CEO for making this dream become a reality.

About

Bishop Dickson Juma Omukosi

Bishop Dickson Juma Omukosi was born and raised in a remote area of Kenya, where he learned that prayer and scripture was the answer to change his story. Bishop Omukosi believes through prayer, all things are possible and can be accomplished. He demonstrates that in his debut book, "Change My Story Oh Lord, Change - Powerful Prayers and Scriptures to Change Your Destiny."

As 1 of 21 children, Bishop Omukosi accepted God at a young age, answering the call to be a prophet, preach the word of God and act as an intercessor. He has over 20 years in ministry and has been a Bishop for 13 years with 20 churches that serve under him.

Bishop Omukosi is the founder of Zion - The Mountain of Deliverance Ministries, Int'l with branches around the globe. He can be compared to the prophet Elijah as a man of a few words, carrying the mantle of prayer. Bishop Omukosi is founder of the Elijah Prayer Network, which is moving nations in prayer and during prayer summits.

Introduction

All scripture was taken from the New International Version of the Bible except where noted.

Prayer is the direct communication a man or woman has to always have with his maker. Prayer has to be and must be a lifestyle of any Christian for it is by prayer that things do change.

For Christians to get to the spiritual realm, prayer gives access to the spiritual and then back to the physical. The Bible says the prayers of the righteous availeth much...pray on, child of God, and keep on praying without ceasing. Our God calls us to pray.

Mathew 7:7: "Ask and it will be given to you; seek and you will find; knock and the door will be opened to you."

Jeremiah 33:3: "Call unto me and I shall answer thee and show you great and wonderful things which you know not."

Our God is calling us into prayer, child of God. There is no one in the Bible who walked with God that was not a person of prayer. If there is one who prays, we have a God who answers our prayers.

- Noah prayed and God answered
- Abraham prayed and God answered
- Isaac prayed and God answered
- Jacob prayed and God answered
- Elijah prayed and God answered
- Solomon prayed and God answered

This is proof-positive that our God is ready and willing to answer your prayers, even now.

Preface

Born and raised in the African nation of Kenya has steered me towards a robust prayer life more than anything else. You can be distracted looking for materialistic things and end up not enjoying it at all. From the beginning, we were all protected by our Father, who knew well the dangers that we were facing, were going to face, or would face in the future. My family of 21 siblings was not a joke; witchcraft was everywhere, and this made me into a prayer warrior.

In 2010, I went into a Daniel kind of fasting mode away from home into the wilderness asking God for a breakthrough and the tables in our family to be turned into blessings since all of us were just caught in the snares, charms, and witchcraft of all nature. We overcame and now the church which I head is built on the foundation of prayer. After 21 days of prayer and fasting, God answered my prayers and there was a great manifestation in our family and almost all of our family members are now witnesses, testifying to the work of the Lord.

I have seen the Lord changing lives, marriages, businesses, just after prayer; remember, every other person on earth is going through something. Just call upon the name of the Lord and you shall be saved. People are now praying and believing in God for a great movement, wonderful breakthroughs, and blessings of our heavenly Father.

God has called me into the prophetic and sends me to nations as it is written in Matthew 10:8: "Heal the sick, raise the dead, cleanse those who have leprosy, drive out demons. Freely you have received; freely give." Nations are beginning to understand the power of prayer when we come together for God says in Matthew 18:20, "For where two or three gather in my name, there am I with them."

Intentionally Left Blank

CHAPTER 1

CALLED TO PRAY

As Christians, we are all called to pray. We follow Jesus Christ, the son of the living God, who was all about prayer. The Bible says in Matthew, every evening, Jesus went away into the mountains to pray. Look here, child of God, He prayed *every evening*. If our Lord and Savior prayed every evening, and the Bible says pray without ceasing, what of us complaining, giving up on praying, and so on?

James 5:13: "Is anyone among you in trouble? Let them pray. Is anyone happy? Let them sing songs of praise."

We are called to pray since the world in which we live is now full of threats, terror, and rejection. As it's written in 2 Timothy 3:1: "But mark this: There will be terrible times in the last days."

Exodus 3:7: The Lord said, "I have indeed seen the misery of my people in Egypt. I have heard them crying out because of their slave drivers, and I am concerned about their suffering."

Child of God, Israelites prayed to their God to save them from their taskmaster and the Lord heard it and came down to deliver them from the land of slavery. You need to pray for your freedom and pray for your deliverance, for God has called us into prayer.

Reflect on *Jeremiah* 33:3: "Call to me and I will answer you and tell you great and unsearchable things you do not know." He has called us to pray, so let's bring him into our midst and into every situation for He never changes at all. Prayer must become a lifestyle for all Christians, since God says I was waiting to hear you pray but you didn't pray. Let us not be too busy for God. He is waiting for you to pray so that He can answer. The Israelites prayed since they knew no one else could get them out of slavery but only God. Some situations won't change until you bring in the game-changer.

The Bible says that the Lord has put watchmen over the walls of Jerusalem who shall not slumber but will keep on reminding them of His promises. I hope you are among the watchmen chosen by God over the walls of your family, the walls of your business, and the walls over your ministry. Don't slumber; keep on reminding Him of His promises.

Let us pray:

You are a faithful God. Remind us that you are in control as we choose to trust you this day. Thank you for being sovereign over my life. We praise you, Father, in Jesus' name, Amen.

Now that I'm called to pray, my Father, my Father, thank you for the grace you have given me. I use it now to declare my season of abundance, victory, and breakthroughs are here now in Jesus' name. I shall walk and operate under open heavens in Jesus' name.

Philippians 4:19: "And my God will meet all your needs according to the riches of his glory in

Christ Jesus." *Today I confess that I shall never lack but enjoy the abundance of riches of my Father in heaven, in Jesus' name.*

I confess that I shall not die but live to testify to the goodness of God over my life in Jesus' name, for by the stripes of our Lord Jesus Christ, I'm healed in Jesus' name.

I confess that no weapon formed against me shall prosper in Jesus' name.

I confess that I shall never be broke again for my Father owns silver and gold; my God is rich in His glory.

I confess that I'm moving from one level to another level for the Word of God records that you, Oh Lord, will lift us from one glory to another glory.

I confess that I shall be the head and not the tail, be above and not beneath and lend to nations and not borrow, in Jesus' name. (Duet. 28:14)

I confess that I shall not fight in any battle; my God, the creator of heaven and the earth, will fight every battle and give me victory in Jesus' name. (2 Chronicles 20)

I confess that it shall never be forsaken by my God and my kids will never beg for bread in Jesus' name, for the Lord is my shepherd.

Except the Lord built the house, they labour in vain that built it: except the Lord keeps the city, the watchman waketh but in vain. (Psalm 127: 1)

Though I walk in the midst of trouble, thou will revive me. Thou will stretch forth thy hand against the wrath of my enemies, and thy right hand shall save me. (Psalm 138:7)

For thou hast delivered my soul from death: wilt thou not deliver my feet from falling, that I may walk before God in the light of the living? (Psalm 56:13)

The Lord is my rock and my fortress and my deliverer; my God, my strength, in whom will I trust;

my buckler and the horn of my salvation, and my high tower. (Psalm 18:2)

The Lord is on my side; I will not fear! What can man do unto me? (Psalm 118:6)

Blessed be the Lord, my strength, which teacheth my hands to war and my fingers to fight. (Psalm 144:1)

When my enemies are turned back, they shall fall and perish at thy presence. (Psalm 9:3)

Notes

Notes

CHAPTER 2

COMMAND YOUR DAY

In Psalm 30:5, weeping may endure for a night, but joy comes in the morning. Some things happen in our life because we have not taken hold or control of our day. We let the devil and the dark world rule over us. An enlightened Christian will always wake up early in the morning to take control of their day. Reflect on Job 38:12. Have you commanded your morning and have you placed your dawn where it belongs? For a fruitful day, it should begin with prayer. The Bible records that the enemy comes to sow evil seeds, therefore, we need to take charge of our day.

Commanding your day includes praying and asking God to bring good people into your day, lined with blessings, and ready to be a blessing to you in Jesus' name. It's all about going to the throne of mercy before they go to their shrines of darkness.

Before the sun rises, I speak to it to bring good tiding, to bring healing, and cause my enemies to scatter. In Exodus, the Lord told Moses to go early in the morning to the river Nile before Pharaoh gets there. Why? The king of Egypt had idol gods in the river Nile. So in other words, God is telling Moses to go and destroy the gods of pharaoh so that the supernatural can take control. God -- IAM that IAM -- is glorified.

When you command your day, plans of the wicked fail and the Lord takes charge of your whole day; that is why He says in Jeremiah 33:3 to call unto Me and I shall answer thee and show you great and mighty things which you know not. There are things that the devil has planned, and we know not, so when we call on Him, He reveals them to us, and we overcome them.

Prayers To Command Your Morning:

- I command the morning to take hold of the ends of the earth and shake the wicked out of it as it is written in Job 38:12, in Jesus' name.
- Release the beauty of Your holiness from the womb of the morning (Ps. 110:3) today in Jesus' name.
- Let Your light break forth in my life as the morning (Ps. 58:8) has done in Jesus' name.
- Let Your judgments come upon the enemy morning by morning as it is written in Isa. 28:19, in Jesus' name.
- Lord, You prepared the morning, and I pray that You will come as the rain, the latter and former rain upon the earth today in Jesus' name. (Hos. 6:3)
- I will not be afraid of the arrow that flies by day or the terror that comes at night. (Ps. 91:5)

- I take authority over every demon that is released against me and my family at night to cause stagnation, death, and troubles in Jesus' name.
- I bind and take authority over all nightmares and demonic dreams at night that will bring troubles in the day in the name of Jesus.
- I draw upon heavenly resources today, in the name of Jesus.
- I confess that this is the day that the Lord has made; I will rejoice and be glad in it, in the name of Jesus.
- I decree that all the elements of this day will cooperate with me, in the name of Jesus.
- I decree that these elemental forces will refuse to cooperate with my enemies this day, in the name of Jesus.
- I speak unto you the sun, the moon, and the stars; you will not smite me and my family this day, in the name of Jesus.

- I pull down every negative energy planning to operate against my life this day, in the name of Jesus.
- I dismantle any power that is uttering incantations to capture this day, in the name of Jesus.
- I render null and void such incantations and satanic prayers over me and my family, in the name of Jesus.
- I retrieve this day out of their hands, in the name of Jesus.
- I program blessings unto the sun, the moon and the stars for my life today, in the name of Jesus.
- Oh sun, cancel every daily evil program drawn against me, in the name of Jesus.
- Oh sun, moon and stars, fight against the stronghold of witchcraft targeted against me today, in the name of Jesus.

- You, the sun, moon and stars, you shall favor me today, in the name of Jesus.
- Every evil arrangement prepared by the sorcerers and witches against my life today, let them scatter and die, in the name of Jesus.
- Any evil thing that will be programmed into the sun, the moon and the stars against my life today, be dismantled, in the name of Jesus.
- I shake off every season of frustration and failure, in the name of Jesus.
- I refuse to give a reply to any satanic programming against my life today, in Jesus' name.
- Every wicked war working against me in the heavenlies, I overthrow you, in the name of Jesus.
- I stand against every satanic operation that would hinder my prayers today, in the name of Jesus.
- Every wicked spirit's plans to rob me of the will of God, fall down and die, in the name of Jesus.

- I tear down the stronghold of Satan against my life, in the name of Jesus.
- Today, I refuse to be in the right place at the wrong time, in Jesus' name.
- I bind every negative energy in the air, water, and ground working against me, in the name of Jesus.
- Anything from the kingdom of darkness that has made it their business to hinder me, I single you out right now and bind you, in the name of Jesus.
- I recover all my virtues dedicated to the elements in the name of Jesus.
- Let the heavens declare the glory of God over my life, in the name of Jesus.
- Everything programmed into my life in the heavenlies, I dismantle you, in the name of Jesus.
- Spirit of favor, counsel, might, and power, come upon me, in the name of Jesus.
- I shall excel this day and nothing shall defile me, in the name of Jesus.

- I shall possess the gates of my enemies this day, in the name of Jesus.
- The Lord shall anoint me with the oil of gladness above my fellows this day, in the name of Jesus.
- The fire of the enemy will not burn me and my family this day, in the name of Jesus.
- My ears shall hear good news and I shall not hear the voice of the enemy today, in the name of Jesus.
- My life and the lives of the members of my family are secured in Christ, in the name of Jesus.
- Let every satanic check point mounted against me in the heavenlies be dismantled by the Word of the Lord, in Jesus' name.
- Every evil altar prepared against my breakthroughs in the heavenlies, and in the sea, be dismantled by fire, in the name of Jesus.
- I command spiritual wickedness militating against me, I bring the hook of the Lord

against you and frustrate your activities, in Jesus' name.

- I receive open heavens for my life this day, in Jesus' name.
- I take divine insurance against all forms of accident and tragedy, in the name of Jesus.
- I send lightning, thunder, and the hook of the Lord against the evil queen in the heavenlies militating against me, in the name of Jesus.
- Every evil spiritual equation programmed against my life, I command you to change, in Jesus' name.
- I speak unto the headquarters of evil programmers and blow up their altars, in the name of Jesus.
- Anything drawing power against me from the heavenlies, fall down and die, in the name of Jesus.

Notes

CHAPTER 3

RESTORATION PRAYERS

When the enemy comes in, his goal is always to steal, kill and destroy (John 10:10), but when you continue with that scripture, you will find that Jesus says, "I have come that they may have life, and have it to the full." Let that be your testimony! In Jesus' name, you will have life and life more abundantly.

Restoration is all about what you had before but the enemy has taken it from you either legally or illegally, as we know the work of the enemy is to steal, kill and destroy so whatever thing that you used to have and it's no more, just know that someone is responsible for that; therefore, you need to rise and claim your blessings, breakthrough, marriages back in Jesus' name. Through Joel the prophet of God, the Lord promises restoration of years. (Joel 2)

In Genesis 1, when the Lord our God made man and woman, he made him in His image -- strong, genius, blessed as the Lord himself. But when we get to Chapter 2 of Genesis, the devil comes to get them away from God, to destroy the relationship, and destroy the fellowship. This is the work of the enemy.

Destruction

Jesus Christ restored the lost glory back to man by giving power back to us, to walk over snakes and scorpions; the serpent that destroyed the fellowship of man and his maker; now you got the power over him. Luke 10:19: I have given you authority to trample on snakes and scorpions and to overcome all the power of the enemy; nothing will harm you. You got the power to rise! Don't lose it and just sit there waiting. David, when he lost it, went to God to inquire if he can catch up with the enemies and restore whatever that was stolen from him. (1 Samuel 30)

Prayers For Restoration:

- Father God as you restored Job your servant, I pray today that the Lord restores to me everything which I've lost to my enemies in Jesus' name.

- As you commanded the wife of Abraham to be restored, command my blessings which someone is using to be restored now by an offering of trespass in Jesus' name.

- Father, you promised in Joel 2:25 I will repay you for the years the locusts have eaten — the great locust and the young locust, the other locusts and the locust swarm -- my great army that I sent among you. I pray today that my Father restores to me more and more years wasted away so that I may recover and restore everything which I've lost in Jesus' name.

- Restore to me my lost glory, my position, and Daddy, make me shine again in Jesus' name.

- Father, I thank you for the restoration of my past glory in Jesus' name.
- Lord, let there be all-around restoration in my life through this prayer, in the name of Jesus.
- I command all evil unknown forces organized against my life to be scattered, in the name of Jesus.
- I recover all my blessings that I had lost to the enemy, in Jesus' name.
- I bind the spirit of stagnation, frustration and disillusionment in my life, in the name of Jesus.
- I command all the damages done to my life by household enemies to be repaired, in the name of Jesus.
- I command all doors of good things closed against me by the enemy to be opened, in the name of Jesus.
- I reject the spirit of impossibility; I claim open doors, in the name of Jesus.

- I decree restoration seven-fold in all areas of my life, in the name of Jesus.
- Lord, give me the solution to any problem facing me, in the name of Jesus.
- I possess the power to pursue, overtake, and recover my goods from spiritual Egyptians, in the name of Jesus.
- Lord, heal me and restore me totally in Jesus' name.
- Let all hidden potential and gifts that will make me great, and that which was stolen from me, be restored a hundred-fold, in the name of Jesus.
- I reject the spirit of poverty, lack, and want in the name of Jesus.
- Every evil agent who has taken what belongs to me, I command them to release it in Jesus' name.
- I retrieve back from the hands of the enemy any of my possessions that I unknowingly misplaced, in Jesus' name.

- I recover all the ground that I had lost to the enemy, in Jesus' name.
- I command sevenfold restoration of everything the enemy has taken from me, in Jesus' name.
- Oh Lord, restore my wasted years, in Jesus' name.
- Lord, restore my wasted efforts, money, health, strength and blessings, in Jesus' name.
- I break in pieces every covenant or curse obstructing divine restoration in my life, in Jesus' name.
- I command a hundred-fold restoration of everything the enemy took from me when I was weak, in Jesus' name.
- I destroy by the Holy Ghost fire the four horns assigned to scatter my prosperity, family, business and possessions, in Jesus' name.

- Every good thing God has destined for me, but is in the possession of someone else, I command it to come to me now, in Jesus' name.
- I possess the power to pursue, overtake, and recover my goods from agents of darkness, in the name of Jesus.
- Lord, heal all wounds and spiritual brokenness sustained from attacks of the enemy in Jesus' name.
- Father, I pray, remove any evil man or woman sitting on my blessings, miracles, breakthrough, prosperity, finance, job or good health, in the name of Jesus Christ.
- All my possessions lost in the north, south, east or west, I command them to come to me now, in Jesus' name.
- All my possessions in the spirit realm, I release them into the physical by fire, in the name of Jesus Christ.

- I receive a hundredfold restoration of everything the enemy stole from me, in the name of Jesus Christ.

Notes

Notes

CHAPTER 4

PRAYER PETITIONS

Have you ever had some accusations against you which were not good at all? Or maybe you heard of some rulings about people and felt no, that was not fair. Now petitioning is all about unjust rulings or happenings that are not good at all for you, your family, job or anything that concerns you.

In 2017, we held an election in my country where the sitting president was contesting against the opposition leader -- the former prime minister. The voting was done peacefully and results were announced in favor of the sitting head of state. The former prime minister who was the opposition leader rejected the results and said it was his victory, and it has been stolen from him. He decided to go to the supreme court to petition and the ruling was done in his favor and the court ordered the repeat of the elections.

This gives you the picture of a prayer petition which you ought to do. Go for what rightfully belongs to you.

The Bible says that Abraham petitioned God on Sodom and Gomorrah and

God listened for God had made up His mind on the destruction of Sodom and Gomorrah even without saving Lot and his family. You can, therefore, stand in the gap for those whom you love for God to intervene on their behalf. That barren woman whom you know of, that old man who has been denied his rights, that widow suffering or being oppressed with her people -- you need to stand in the gap and petition on their behalf for God to deliver, help, or raise them up from the trouble.

In Genesis 25:21, after Isaac learned that his wife Rebecca was barren, he decided to petition God over the issue since he was the son of the covenant.

Rebecca was out of options to give birth; all avenues had been exhausted and Isaac knew it was not yet over until God took over. The Bible says Isaac petitioned God. You need to boldly approach his throne of mercy as a son or daughter, an heir in the kingdom, and petition for your rightful position and blessings.

After Hezekiah was told by the prophet of God who was sent to him by God to put his house in order for, he was going to die, the man didn't agree with the sentence of God; he thought the ruling was not fair and he decided to remind God of his wonderful works he had done. God remembered and added 15 years to his life. The Bible says his mercies surpass His judgment; just seek His mercies like Hezekiah, though He has ruled in his anger but with His mercies, all shall be turned around.

The daughters of Zelophehad petitioned Moses in the entrance of the tent of meeting and gave him a story of their family; they had no male child and their father was dead; now all the inheritance that belonged to them was being taken away since they were but only daughters and no son. It was a rule in Israel that if a man dies and has no son, his inheritance is taken away by the relatives. So they decided to petition God through his servant Moses that the rule has to be changed to let them have their father's inheritance. The Bible says that Moses presented the matter before God and God said do what the Zelophehad daughters wanted, and it was turned, and they got their father's inheritance.

Don't just let it go. Go after what rightly belongs to you.

Pray these prayers:

- Oh God, my Father, I pray today God changes my story; I'm so low, I've become the laughingstock in every council of the scornful. Father, make me laugh again, in Jesus' name.

- As the Bible encourages us, Isaac prayed and you blessed his wife with twin children; I pray today that my father sees my case is urgent, I need double for my trouble. I've suffered enough, gone through enough issues now.

- Lord, change my story, in Jesus' name.

- I turn tables upside down today and claim my victory, claim my blessings and call on the fire of the Holy Ghost to burn and destroy all evil charms working against me, in Jesus' name.

- I'm an heir to your kingdom, oooh Lord, and in this hour, my life is in shambles, struggle after struggle. This is not my inheritance. Someone has taken my position and rights. I overthrow everyone sitting in my glory as I take back my position, in Jesus' name.

- As you opened the womb of Rachel, I pray today, oooh God, open my womb and let me bear my fruits, let me get my job, let me shine in my area of calling, in Jesus' name.

- I know I sinned and qualified for the sentence that you have pronounced against me but Lord, you called me to come reason together with You. I've come Father; forgive me and have mercy upon me and deliver me, in Jesus' name. Lord, change your verdict on my matter today, in Jesus' name.

- I pray a prayer of Hezekiah, Lord; remember all that I've done in your kingdom; redeem some days for me. Deliver and make me whole, in Jesus' name.
- May you change my story as you changed that one of Ruth, David, and Elisha and make me into one you celebrate and testify about all the time as you testified about David, in Jesus' name.
- Enough of this barrenness. I call forth my children from the north, east, west and the south, in Jesus' name.
- My pockets are dry, my life is not moving on well. Father, change my life.
- Bless the work of my hands and do your Word, in Jesus' name.
- Oh Lord, I have cried for so long; put a smile on my face by blessing me with children.
- Unto thee oh Lord do I put my hope and trust; do not let me be ashamed. Never let my enemies laugh at me and ask me where is my God?

- You are the giver of children; you blessed Hannah with Samuel and Sarah with Isaac. Bless me with mine, Lord Oh Lord, settle me in this marriage and make me a mother to my biological children, in Jesus' name.

- Your word says in Jeremiah 29:11: "For I know the thoughts that I think towards you, the thoughts of peace and not of evil to give you a future and a hope." I know your thoughts towards me aren't barrenness, unemployment, or poverty; therefore, open doors and make a way for me to rejoice again, in Jesus' name.

- Lord Jesus, on the cross of Calvary you said, "it is finished" and that includes my pains and sorrow. Right now, Lord, wipe away these tears from my eyes.

- Bless me and turn around my situation for your glory, in Jesus' name.

- Children are a heritage from God. Psalm 127:3: "Behold, children are a heritage from the Lord, the fruit of the womb is His reward." (KJV). Lord, I need my heritage; give them to me in Jesus' name.

- My mother and my in-laws yearn to carry their grandchildren. Lord Jesus, take this shame away from me and help me to grant their hearts' desires.

- I depend only on you omniscient God; I have no other God besides you. Give me a reason to smile again, in Jesus' name.

- Who can speak when the Lord has not spoken? Pure Father of light, go now and destroy every evil voice that is speaking louder than your voice over my life, husband, and my fruitfulness, in the name of Jesus.

- I believe the report of the Almighty God, therefore, I can cancel every evil report over my life, my business, and my ministry, in the name of Jesus Christ.

- Every arrow of miscarriage, failed pregnancy, and barrenness fired into my life by the power of Satan, in the name of Jesus, backfire, in Jesus' name.

- Father, I cry out to you Lord; show me mercy. Let the sound of joy be heard in my household, in Jesus' name.
- By the blood of Jesus Christ that speaks better things than the blood of Abel, I erase every negative word that has been spoken over my life as I begin to prophesy positivity into my life.
- I know, Lord, that I am a sinner and in diverse ways, I have fallen short of your glory. If my dryness, stagnation, rejection is a result of my past sins and ignorance, Father have mercy on me and wipe away my tears, in Jesus' name.
- Change my story and fill my house with laughter; let all that laughed at me come and laugh with me. I ask this through Christ Jesus.

Notes

CHAPTER 5

FAMILY AND SELF DELIVERANCE

The family forms an important component in society and ministry as well, but it cannot be of importance if it's tied up, locked up, or operating on curses and evil torments. People are stagnant, just failing, suffering from premature death, and being laid off from jobs so easily, even without a cause. One must realize the need for deliverance and prayer before the whole family is destroyed.

The Bible says in Isaiah 51:1, "Hearken to me ye that follow after righteousness, ye that seek the Lord: look unto the rock from which you were hewn, and the quarry from which you were dug." Some of the trouble some people have is in their blood; that rejection is in the family bloodline; that stagnation is in the family bloodline; that sickness is in the family bloodline, since it's in all of the family members.

You are under a lot of pressure wherever you go -- recurring illnesses, a lot of debt, rejection, stagnation, troubled marriage, short temperance, poverty, and evil dreams, and on and on. You may be thinking, why is it that people I trained with are settled? Why are they working, but me, I'm not working? My peers are all settled in marriages; why not me?

I know these questions might be in your mind, but listen the only way out is through prayers. The Bible says pray without ceasing.

It's only prayer that will get you out of your troubled life. When you pray, heaven responds, when you pray, angels are released to your aid. When you pray, the Lord our God answers by fire. When you pray, situations change. **Consider prayers.**

In James 5:13, Is anyone among you troubled, let him pray. Therefore pray. Let prayers be your lifestyle, child of God, even before you get into trouble. Learn to invest in prayers ahead of you so that before anything happens, there's already a way out of your troubles.

Some people have given up already. Families have given up and this has allowed too much to happen in their lives, which makes their dwelling place a place of comfort for the devil to reside and succeed so much so, they end up now becoming witches, people who curse others that are succeeding in life. It always happens like that; when others are thriving and you are struggling, you will always start cursing them, calling them names, when you know for real where it all went wrong. Pray without ceasing. That sickness is not normal, the way things are happening in your family is not normal. Turn around and turn it to God via prayers.

Some of these troubles in the family might be brought into our lives through:

1. Evil altars
2. Witchcraft
3. Assimilations
4. Family Bloodlines

5. Continental, countries, regional, villages evil territorial warlords.

Prayers for the Family:

- Oooh deliver my family from every witchcraft bewitchment, in the name of Jesus Christ.

- Every witchcraft chants, spells and projections made against me and my family, I bind it now and turn it back to the sender, in Jesus' name.

- I frustrate every plot, device, scheme and projection of witchcraft designed to affect any area in my life, in Jesus' name.

- Every damage done to our destinies through witchcraft operations be reversed now and everything works for us, in Jesus' name.

- Any witchcraft covenant done where our blessings, destines are hidden be broken now and completely be destroyed, in Jesus' name.

- Oh Lord, I thank you for your love and peace upon my life; all the glory to you in the mighty name of Jesus Christ. Father, I appreciate you for your power and grace upon my life; to you be all the glory and honor, in the mighty name of Jesus Christ.

- Oh Lord, I ask for your mercy in all ways I have sinned against you and fallen short of your glory; please forgive me and have mercy upon me, in the mighty name of Jesus Christ. Father, in all ways, I have brought myself into this bondage; please forgive me and deliver me by your mighty power, in Jesus' mighty name.

- Oh Lord my Father, deliver me from every satanic stronghold I have found myself, in the mighty name of Jesus Christ.

- Every stronghold of poverty and lack, oh Lord, deliver me from them all, in the mighty name of Jesus Christ.

- Every bondage of stagnation and limitation, Father let your fire deliver me now, in the mighty name of Jesus Christ.

- Every wall built against my progress in the spirit realm, I command you to fall and crumble now, in the mighty name of Jesus Christ.

- Household enemies exchanging my glory for their children, I command you to release my glory now by fire, in the mighty name of Jesus Christ.

- Every satanic bondage I have put myself in through the words of my mouth, Oh Lord, let your mighty hand deliver me now, in the mighty name of Jesus Christ.

- Every satanic prison that my parents and guardians have put me through -evil covenants and unfulfilled promises, I set myself free now, by the power in the blood of Jesus Christ.

- Every bondage I have kept myself in through the unholy relationships I have kept in the past, I set myself loose now, by the blood of Jesus Christ

- Stronghold of masturbation and sexual addiction, break from my life now by fire, in the mighty name of Jesus Christ.

- Satanic force dragging me back from the fulfillment of my destiny, receiving the judgment of fire now, in the mighty name of Jesus Christ.

- You, an evil dream that has been projected against my fulfillment and joy in my career, I destroy your powers over my life, in the mighty name of Jesus Christ.

- Every charm used against me to cause me disfavor in the presence of my helpers, I command it to expire by fire, in the mighty name of Jesus Christ.

- Altars of witches raised against my destiny, catch fire and burn to ashes now, in the mighty name of Jesus Christ.

- Every spirit of error projected into my life, I command you to get out by fire, in the mighty name of Jesus Christ.

- Satanic personalities arranged from the pit of hell against my career, I command you to die by fire, in the mighty name of Jesus Christ.

- Mirrors of darkness used to monitor and regulate my life, break into pieces now, in the mighty name of Jesus Christ.

- Powers of hell making enchantments against my marriage, I command your enchantments to backfire, in the mighty name of Jesus Christ.

- Powers of my adversary, I render you useless upon my life and family, in the mighty name of Jesus Christ.

- I decree that all my plans shall succeed, and I shall be celebrated, in the mighty name of Jesus Christ.

- I release myself from every ancestral connection negatively affecting my Christian life, in the name of Jesus.

- I release myself from every demonic connection emanating from my parents' religion that is negatively affecting my life, in the name of Jesus.

- I release myself from demonic connection emanating from my past involvement in any demonic religion, in the name of Jesus.

- I break and loose myself from every form of sin that is affecting my Christian testimony, in the name of Jesus.
- Let every enemy of my life and destiny seeking my downfall be completely destroyed by the power in the blood of the Lord Jesus.
- By the power of the Holy Spirit, I place my flesh under subjection in the name of Jesus.
- My Father continually delivers me from all forms of temptation in the name of Jesus.
- I purge myself from every evil deposit of the devil, in the name of Jesus.
- Let all negative materials circulating in my bloodstream be flushed out by the blood of Jesus, in the name of Jesus.
- Father, let your anointing flow from the crown of my head to the sole of my feet, breaking every yoke of bondage in my life, in Jesus' name.

- I cut myself off from every spirit of lust in Jesus' name. I cut myself off from every seducing spirit, in the name of Jesus.

- Holy Ghost fire, purge my life in Jesus' name.

- I claim my complete deliverance, in the name of Jesus, from all demonic spirits in Jesus' name.

- I break the hold of any evil power over my life, in Jesus' name.

Notes

Notes

CHAPTER 6

BREAKING THE CHAINS OF STAGNATION

Stagnation is a state of no progress or no real movement in the right direction or slow progress. Here is where one says in his heart that the Lord left me, or it may be said the person has sinned to be in this state. Nothing good seems to be happening; everything you do seems to come to nothing and people around you are expecting you to progress in life. Someone is educated but has nothing to show for the years he was in school -- no job, no marriage, no child -- no progress at all. This state makes one feel too low and even sends one into rejection -- self-rejection, where one hides from people and does not feel important.

Duet 2:3: The Lord commands Moses to tell the children of Israel that as you have compassed this mountain, it's enough now.

Child of God, stagnation is bad. Demons sometimes make one feel he is progressing only to see that you have just been going around in the same position. The Bible calls them *busy bodies*. People trying to build themselves houses but they never come to completion; some trying to get married, but it never comes to pass.

The same state which your brother or your sisters are in is the same one you are suffering from. The whole family is troubled. Stagnation even can be felt in your family; no one is making progress in life. Be Moses of your family. Be Joseph of your family and pray.

There's a line which is drawn in your life or your family which never allows you to cross to the other end to finish. You need to pray, child of God, for this is now rampant all over-- doing business but making no progress; children are in good schools but making no progress. Arise and pray and break off those chains of stagnation and walk free, in Jesus' name.

Prayers to break stagnation:

- Every yoke of stagnation operating in my life, break by fire, in the name of Jesus.
- Every witchcraft power working against my progress, be destroyed, in Jesus' name.
- Satanic cobwebs from my Father's house, mother's house or from my household that are holding my progress, catch fire, in Jesus' name.
- My tied hands in the realm of the spirit by evil forces, be loosed out, in the name of Jesus.
- The blood of Jesus shall flow through the work of my hands, in the name of Jesus.
- Every generational curse of eating from hand to mouth that has been working in my family, break by fire, in Jesus' name.
- I cast out the monitoring spirit of poverty around my life, in the name of Jesus.

- Any man or woman assigned to pull me down from my ladder of greatness, fall and die, in Jesus' name.
- Every evil pattern of loss, break by fire, in the name of Jesus.
- Every evil load upon my life, I shake you out, in the name of Jesus.
- The anointing of go slow upon my life, expire and be destroyed, in the name of Jesus.
- Powers planted in my childhood to trouble my future, hear the word of the Lord and be destroyed, in Jesus' name.
- I bind the evil power of stagnation in my life, in Jesus' name.
- I will not be a slave to others, in Jesus' name.
- I cancel the dream of poverty, in Jesus' name.
- Every chain of inherited witchcraft in my family, break and catch fire, in Jesus' name.

- Every altar of darkness dragging me backward, catch fire, in Jesus' name
- I receive the double portion of progress, in Jesus' name.
- As from today, everything that concerns my life shall move forward, in Jesus' name.
- I bind every spirit chasing away my miracles, in Jesus' name.
- Every satanic power that wants to glue me to the ground be destroyed and buried by fire, in Jesus' name.
- Fire of deliverance, enter into my life and deliver me from stagnation, in Jesus' name.
- Every spirit of stagnation in my marriage, die, in Jesus' name.
- Every power taking my names to the graveyard, burn to ashes, in Jesus' name.
- Holy Spirit, convert my stagnation to double acceleration, in Jesus' name.
- Every power activating stagnation and delay in my life, die, in Jesus' name.

- Every spiritual chain of slavery upon my life, break. I refuse to remain stagnant in life in Jesus' name.

- My Father, whatever the spirit of stagnation has denied me of, I recover my time, money, and glory, in Jesus' name.

- You, satanic embargo, causing me to remain on one level for many years, I command you to expire by fire, in the mighty name of Jesus Christ. Satanic cage holding back my destiny from breaking forth, I command you to open and release me now by fire, in the mighty name of Jesus Christ.

- Altars of darkness setting limitations for me, my career and health, I command you to be destroyed by fire, now in the mighty name of Jesus Christ.

- Every curse placed upon my life from an infant that is causing me stagnation, I break the giver of that soul curse now; you shall no longer prosper in my life, in the mighty name of Jesus Christ.

- Oh Lord, I receive speed to move beyond where I am right now, in the mighty name of Jesus Christ.
- I decree that everything I have lost due to stagnation shall be restored speedily, in the mighty name of Jesus Christ.
- I receive advancement in all areas of my life and family, in the mighty name of Jesus Christ.
- I decree that the yoke of stagnation and limitation is broken in my life totally, in the mighty name of Jesus Christ.
- I break up every yoke of the enemy over my finances, in the mighty name of Jesus Christ.
- I command every yoke of limitation over my health to be broken now, in the mighty name of Jesus Christ.
- I cross every line of limitations set against my life and family members, in the mighty name of Jesus Christ.
- Every spiritual cage where I am being kept in order to restrict my progress, I break free

from the cage now, in the mighty name of Jesus Christ.

- Every satanic manipulation causing stagnation in my marriage, I command you to end right now, in the mighty name of Jesus Christ.

- I decree that I shall no longer remain on one spot in destiny; I shall begin to move on speedily, in the mighty name of Jesus.

- Evil cobwebs that used to tie me down in life, I command you to catch fire, in the mighty name of Jesus Christ.

- The powers of darkness assigned against my next level be destroyed by fire, in the mighty name of Jesus Christ.

- I decree that I shall no longer remain in the same spot in my office; I receive promotion now, in the mighty name of the Lord Jesus Christ.

- Powers gathered against my promotion were destroyed by fire, in the mighty name of Jesus Christ.

- Household enemies that have vowed that I will be limited in life, be judged by fire, in the mighty name of Jesus Christ.
- I command everything in creation to begin to work in favor of my advancement now, in the mighty name of Jesus Christ.
- Father, I receive supernatural speed now to recover all that I have lost in times past, in the mighty name of Jesus Christ.
- Powers of hell gathered against my freedom and growth, I command you to scatter by fire, in the mighty name of Jesus Christ.
- Angels of blessings, locate me now and bless every work of my hands, in the mighty name of Jesus Christ.
- I decree that henceforth, I shall move from one level of greatness to another -- no more limitations, delays and stagnation, in the mighty name of Jesus Christ.
- Every mountain on my way to success and victory, be removed in Jesus' name.

- I destroy by fire every limitation the enemy has marked down for me, in Jesus' name, and I break self-imposed stagnancy and limitations, in the name of Jesus Christ.
- Every spirit of stagnancy, I reject you and I bind you. Like Elisha, I receive a double portion of Your anointing and blessings in exchange for my shame and delay, in Jesus' name.
- Every curse that I have brought into my life through disobedience and ignorance, break by fire, in the name of Jesus Christ.
- Every unspoken curse against my life, family, education, marriage, ministry, employment, career, business and destiny be broken now by the blood of Jesus.
- I release from my life every cycle of failure, disappointments, sickness, and frustration, in Jesus' name.
- I declare and decree that I am delivered, and I am free from every chain, bondage, affliction, curse, limitations, stagnancy, failure and

generational sicknesses and situations in the name of Jesus Christ, the Son of the Living God whose blood breaks every bondage, in Jesus' name. AMEN.

Notes

CHAPTER 7

SPIRIT OF DELAY

Many people are held up and can't progress nor get to their destinies. The devil has held them up and they know it or don't know that this is surely the devil. As from the beginning, I've stated more than once that the work of the devil is to steal, kill and destroy as it is recorded in John 10:10.

Delay is a state in which it takes too long for an accomplishment of something. It takes more time than usual. Delay is far more different from stagnation, for one is for some time while another can take a whole lifetime.

Many have said delay is not denial and I agree with this 100% as many times God uses delay...

1. To prepare us
2. To wait until you attain a state of maturity
3. To make sure that before you get there, all is prepared and ready

4. To remove evil around you
5. To confuse enemies

Before God takes you to another level, sometimes He makes you look confused and distraught which makes the enemy think that you are completely left alone.

Types Of Delay

- Divine delay - caused by the Almighty God
- Self-delay - could be caused by your own action, mistake or error
- Programmed delay - could be programmed into your life by envious enemy
- Bloodline or inherited delay - When you inherit it from your bloodline, parents
- Regional delay - When witches in your environment do not allow people to progress
- Strongman delay - When a strongman has vowed that you will not make it

When you read Exodus 14, we see how God used delay as a tactic to punish the Egyptian soldiers who were coming after the child of God, the Israelites. They thought that God took them from captivity, yet they were held up and couldn't cross the red sea; this was a delay to receive instruction.

At times when people see you are not moving, they always rush to conclude that God left you, you sinned, or you never prayed again. Child of God, delay can make you give up, but I kindly ask you never to give up, but pray on.

Stagnation and delay combined look exactly like a curse; one has to pray and pray more. It's either demonic, an altar, or it's in your bloodline that is making or bringing the happening of stagnation and delay. Abraham, he was held up, stationed, or delayed with no child for a long time; Isaac suffered the same delay; Jacob suffered the same delay and the Israelites also were delayed to come out of slavery, even after God promised only 400 years but 40 years was almost added.

Stagnation also falls into the same category as delay; it is either demonic, coming from the altar that is evil somewhere, or it's in the bloodline as I've mentioned above in the lineage of Abraham. One seems to be going round and round at the same place. When you read Duet 2:3, God had to command the children of Israel to stop going round and round that mountain but rather move northward. Child of God, your time and moment might be here. It's surely your season but it takes longer than expected for you to cross the line. You, therefore, need to pray more and more.

You work but there's no progress, no development, and if there's any, you did it with too much struggle since these spirits were working against you.

The bible records in Ephesians 6 to put on the whole armor of God to be able to resist all the evil arrows. Arise child of God; let's fight for what belongs to us; let's go for it and let's break through.

Are you expecting a promotion in your office, but it is not yet forthcoming?

Are you mature enough to get married, but the right partner is not yet forthcoming?

Are you seeking admission to a university or college, but your application is being rejected, despite the fact that this is your 99th attempt?

Is it taking you too many years to complete or buy your dream house, despite the fact that you are putting in more effort?

Are you expecting a miracle or breakthrough in any area of your life, but it is not manifesting?

Are you expecting a contract but approval was turned down several times and you noticed that your colleagues that are not good enough on the job are being awarded the contracts meant for you?

Prayers for Delay:

- I'm not stagnant or delayed for I am a child of God, and I confess success, breakthrough, and elevation after elevation. Glory to glory, in Jesus' name.

- Delay is not my portion nor stagnation, for I receive the spirit to finish everything with the power of God in Jesus' name.

- I got the power to overtake, not to circle around the circles, and now I move forth by the power of God, in the name of Jesus Christ.

- I break every chain of stagnation and delay in my life in Jesus' name.

- I break every evil covenant of delay in my life right now in Jesus' name.

- Every power bringing or causing delay over everything that I do, I call down the fire of the Holy Ghost to burn it and destroy it in Jesus' name.

- Every altar calling for my delay representing the kingdom of darkness, catch fire and burn to ashes, in Jesus' name.

- Every power prolonging my journey to breakthroughs, fall down and die, in Jesus' name.
- Every problem that I brought into my life through my association with the spirit of delay and frustration die now in Jesus' name.
- I cancel the activities and powers of the spirit of delay in my life, in the name of Jesus.
- I break the covenants and curses of the spirit of delay over my life, in the name of Jesus.
- Every effect of the spirit of delay over my life and that of my family members be nullified by the blood of Jesus.
- Every spirit of sluggishness and backwardness in my life and family members come out of us now and be destroyed, in the name of Jesus.
- Every spirit, preventing good things in my life is destroyed, in the name of Jesus.
- Every evil instruction, prophecy, or predictions issued against my life by demonic utterances be canceled by the blood of Jesus.

- I receive angelic speed to where God wants me to be now as He did to his prophet Elijah, in the name of Jesus.
- Every evil deposit in my life as a result of satanic poison that is bringing delay and stagnation is washed away by the blood of Jesus.
- Lord, catapult me into greatness as You did for Joseph and David, in Jesus' name.
- Let all my enemies and their strongholds be shattered to pieces by the thunder of God, and may it mark my big step to move into my destiny in the name of Jesus.
- I decree that the yoke of stagnation and limitation is broken in my life totally, in the mighty name of Jesus Christ.
- I break up every yoke of the enemy over my finances, my wealth, and financial connections, in the mighty name of Jesus Christ.
- I command every yoke of limitation over my health, my business, and my family to be broken now, in the mighty name of Jesus Christ.

- I cross every line of limitation set against my life and family members, in the mighty name of Jesus Christ.
- Every spiritual cage where I am being kept in order to restrict my progress, I break free from the cage now, in the mighty name of Jesus Christ.
- Every greatness that God has purposed for me and my loved ones, we shall get there, in the mighty name of Jesus Christ.
- Every satanic manipulation causing stagnation in my marriage, I command you to end right now, in the mighty name of Jesus Christ.
- I decree that I shall no longer remain on one point in destiny; I shall begin to move on speedily, in the mighty name of Jesus.
- Evil cobweb used to tie me down in life, I command you to catch fire, in the mighty name of Jesus Christ.

- Powers of darkness assigned against my next level be destroyed by fire, in the mighty name of Jesus Christ.
- Plans of demotion made against me instead of promotion, I command you to scatter by fire, in the mighty name of Jesus Christ.
- I decree that I shall no longer remain in the same office; I receive promotion now, in the mighty name of the Lord Jesus Christ.
- Powers gathered against my promotion were destroyed by fire, in the mighty name of Jesus Christ.
- Household enemies that have vowed that I will be limited in life be judged by fire, in the mighty name of Jesus Christ.
- Father, I receive supernatural speed now to recover all that I have lost in times past, in the mighty name of Jesus Christ.
- Powers of hell gathered against my increase, freedom, and growth, I command you to scatter by fire, in the mighty name of Jesus Christ.

- Angels of blessings, locate me now and bless every work of my hands, in the mighty name of Jesus Christ.
- I decree that henceforth, I shall move from one level of greatness to another-- no more limitation, delay, and stagnation, in the mighty name of Jesus Christ.

Notes

CHAPTER 8

BREAKING THE CURSE OF POVERTY

Poverty is a state in which one cannot even afford simple things or basic things. God is the creator of the universe, and everything in it is very rich. In the Bible it says in Haggai 2 that silver and gold belong to Him; He owns thousands and thousands of bulls on thousands of hills. He is indeed a very rich God.

From Genesis to Revelation, there's no one person written in the Bible who served God diligently with a whole heart and who lived a poor life. They were all rich starting from Noah, Abraham, Isaac, Jacob, Job, and many others; none of them is mentioned as poor. David was so rich! Solomon was rich and in fact, God gave Solomon riches just after prayers.

We have been given the power to become sons of God which means we are the inheritors or heirs in the kingdom of God. All that God has in heaven and stored up here on earth is yours, too. Deuteronomy 8:18 says that He is the Lord our God that gives us power to make wealth.

After you gave your life to Jesus, you became an heir in the kingdom and you were given the power to become rich. Stop living a poor life and complaining. You got the power to unlock riches. In Genesis 26:12, Isaac was struggling a little bit but after following the Word of God and sowing his seeds, the Bible records that he harvested a hundred-fold. Our God has not changed, child of God. He is the same yesterday, today, and forever more. Just pray and work hard.

Some poverty that people go through is inherited. It's in their family's bloodline. Read Isaiah 51:1 -- they were born with it; it's in their blood and it runs in them. Isaac was a blessed man while he was still in the loins of his father Abraham when God blessed him. But this man of God comes and encounters trouble. Poverty can be brought to us due to the regions or areas where we are living.

Poverty is not a permanent state, and this means it can be changed. I always say it's not an error to be born in a poor family but it's an error to die poor. Why? Ecclesiastes 3: there's a time for everything. How are you spending your time? The Bible says the race is not for the swift, so how are you running your race? Work hard and let's see you become big. In Jeremiah 29, God has a plan, which is to prosper you…therefore, you need just to rise and get back to your position as an heir and rich child of God.

God has a plan to prosper you; just tune in and pray these prayers:
- Every witchcraft covenant of poverty affecting my prosperity break, in the name of Jesus.

- Every covenant of poverty made by the living or the dead against my prosperity break, in Jesus' name.
- Hear, oh heavens, I am dead to the covenant of poverty; I am alive to the covenant of prosperity, in Jesus' name.
- Every arrow of poverty fired into my life, come out with all your roots, in the name of Jesus.
- Every curse of poverty placed upon my family, be consumed by fire, in the name of Jesus.
- Every curse of poverty fired into my life by household wickedness, go back to your sender, in Jesus' name.
- Every altar of poverty in my place of birth, working against my prosperity, burn to ashes, in Jesus' name.
- Today, I raise up an altar of continuous prosperity upon my destiny, in the name of Jesus.
- Every stronghold of mental and spiritual poverty in my life, be uprooted by fire, in the name of Jesus

- Any covenant in my life that is strengthening the stronghold of poverty break, in the name of Jesus.
- I bind and cast out every negative word enforcing poverty into my life, in the name of Jesus.
- Every spiritual chain of slavery into poverty upon my life, break by fire, in the name of Jesus.
- Every witchcraft assembly in my neighborhood, be scattered by Holy Ghost fire, in Jesus' name.
- Every witchcraft covenant of poverty affecting my prosperity break, in the name of Jesus.
- Oh Lord, empower me to pluck the seed of wealth that will swallow poverty in my life, in Jesus' name.
- Father Lord, shield me against any arrow of poverty fired against my life, in the name of Jesus.
- Oh Lord, give me divine revelation on my prosperity, in the name of Jesus.

- Oh Lord, let your glory overshadow every work that I do and make me shine in the name of Jesus.
- My star must shine in Jesus' name. I'm walking out of poverty for the glory of God, in Jesus' name.

Notes

Notes

CHAPTER 9

Spiritual Warfare

Sometimes the word **warfare** scares people away, and they tend to think it's about engaging in the physical exchange. No, child of God; it's about spiritual matters. Paul tells us in Ephesians 6:10 that we need to put on the whole armor of God for us to be able to resist the plans of the devil for our battle is not in flesh and blood but against...

- Principalities
- Powers
- Rulers of darkness of this world
- Spiritual wickedness in high places

Now, this forms the basis of our study in this chapter to try to understand that you can't fight the enemy whom you don't know. This means that before we get into a battle or warfare, we must understand who our enemy is. From the beginning, the enemy of man has been known -- the devil. Wherever he is, things never go well. Everything that happens that is not for the glory of God, He must have his hand in. Nothing happens here on earth without a force behind it -- it's either Godly force or an evil force. As explained earlier, the work of the devil is to kill, steal, and destroy but Jesus said he came so that we may have life and have it in abundance.

    Before you engage in any battle, child of God, understand that our enemy is the devil, not that brother you are seeing, not that sister, but the devil. He is only using him or her to accomplish his mission of killing, stealing, and destroying. Jesus told us that if you want to deliver those held by a strong man, go for the big boss; don't waste your time on the small but just their agents.

    Never forget that you are in the army, child of God; that is why our God is called God of heavenly armies. You and I who were given the power to be called the children of God in John 1:12, we are in this army to fight on since the devil doesn't want us to stay connected to our maker, our loving Father; he is at war with us who agree to the Word of God.

In the promises of God to Abraham, he promised him that your generation shall possess the gates of their enemies. Child of God, you can't possess the gates of your enemies without war; for any territory expansion, you need to be ready for war. You are in the army because you got weapons mentioned in the Word which you read and studied every time. The Bible says that our weapons are not carnal; this means we have war.

The serpent who fought in heaven wanting to take the position of God is here with us, the Bible says, walking around, like a roaring lion looking for whom he can devour. Satan is so cunning in a way that he doesn't want the Christian to know the truth but stay in the dark until the end of times. Remember the Bible tells us that, and you will know the truth and the truth shall set you free and the truth is Jesus Christ whom again, the Bible says that when the Son sets you free, you will be free indeed.

Weapons of spiritual warfare:
- a) The blood of Jesus
- b) The Word of God
- c) The name Jesus Christ
- d) Truth
- e) Love

These are the weapons mentioned several times in the Word that a Christian has to apply daily in the war against the devil and his agents. So we fight daily, for the devil is out to make sure that we don't succeed in life, that we never make it to the top, never get married, or our children never make it in life and we remain in his cage, his prison, forever.

He has caged our children on drug addiction; he has chained our sons and daughters on immorality; he has imprisoned some to serve in his kingdom in the dens of alcohol and prostitution; we, therefore, must fight him to set us and others free.

The devil has subdivided his kingdom in 7 God units:

    a)   Kingdom of darkness all over the earth
    b)   Continental control towers or centers
    c)   Countries' command center
    d)   Regional centers
    e)   Village control unit
    f)   Family unit
    g)   Individual level

Therefore, every level has its own strongman or master or commander to carry out the mission as it states in John 10:10, to kill, steal, and destroy. We may be having the same problems but look at yours. It's solvable but to others, it's too hard. A good example is that the whole world experienced inflation. Other nations' economies went down but others survived and are doing well. Why? We come from different continents, regions, and control masters are different.

We might come from the same family but are affected differently. Same mother, same father but the operational grace is different. It is the same with the kingdom of God. Yes, it's the same spirit but different gifts and different manifestations. The mode of fighting may look different, but weapons of warfare are the same for we get them from the Word of God.

Demons operate with terror. That is their language. That is why when you command them to come out of someone, they resist and do want to fight but finally scream and leave. Why? When the lesser power meets the bigger power, the lesser submits and must bow.

Some of us have been misled in this field in the way that we say Christ finished it all. Listen to me, child of God, men and women of God are still preaching today, doing deliverances today; people are still dying today, the devil is still out there fighting today. Remember, Christ said if you desire to follow me then deny yourself, pick up that cross, and follow me. I take this to mean that He came to set an example for us to follow by casting out devils, healing the sick, and delivering the captives.

The devil doesn't want to see you prospering, see you rise to level after level; he rises to fight so you must be prepared to fight child of God; don't just sit there! You got weapons to fight. And whatever he has stolen, go for it and restore.

Do you feel like something is not right somewhere?
Are you going through sickness after sickness? Are you having debt after debt? Child of God, then understand that the devil is ighting you and, therefore, you need to rise and fight back in JESUS' NAME.

Prayers For Spiritual Warfare:

- Father, let every satanic gathering against the gathering of the children of God scatter, in the mighty name of Jesus.
- Father, let every association of demons against the glory of this household scatter by lightning, in the name of Jesus.
- Father, by the Holy Ghost, arise in Your power and wage war against my adversaries, in the name of Jesus.
- Father, by the power of the Holy Ghost, I command you, serpent forces, to vomit everything you have swallowed up in my life, in the name of Jesus.
- Father, show me where the enemy has kept or buried my blessings, in the name of Jesus.
- Father, by the Holy Ghost, arise and chase away every evil dog pursuing me, in the name of Jesus.
- Father, let every power of darkness transacting business underneath great waters release

my virtues, blessings, glory, ministry and calling, in the name of Jesus.

- Father, command my spirit to come out of every satanic prison, in the mighty name of Jesus.
- Father, arise and set my spirit free from the shackles of satanic strongholds, in the name of Jesus.
- Father, I declare today that I deregister my life from the prison of a demonic stronghold and set my life and destiny on the path of progress, in the name of Jesus.
- Father, let every demonic transaction going on in my life and contrary to the will of God for my life be terminated, in the name of Jesus.
- Father, my life is not for sale; I refuse to be sold by any demonic power, in the name of Jesus.
- Father, whoever swallowed my glory and honor, I command them to vomit them by thunder, in the name of Jesus.

- Father, by your consuming fire, let fire go before me and destroy the roundabout of all my enemies, in the name of Jesus.
- Father, let every demonic stranger around me scatter by fire, in the name of Jesus.
- Father, I place my right hand on my head, and I declare that "The power of promotion rests upon me, in the name of Jesus."
- Father, by your mighty power, let all flesh and demons be silenced before you NOW! Speak now and let Your servant hear Your voice, in the name of Jesus.
- Father, by your Word of power, I put a stop to the subtle activity of the devil and his agents against my existence, my family, my career, and all that concerns me, in the name of Jesus.
- Father, Jesus has conquered the world for my sake, therefore, no problem, situation, or the devil has power over me. I receive grace, and I put every devil under my feet, in the mighty name of Jesus.

- Father, I believe the scripture that says, "The Lord will fight for me..." Therefore, I take a stand on that, and I call on God to fight every unseen enemy that is troubling me, in the name of Jesus.
- Father, bless me in all ramifications of life and let the devil and his agents opposing my blessings be brought to judgment, in the mighty name of Jesus.
- Father, I cast down every stronghold of the devil over my life and my moving forward in all aspects of my life, in the name of Jesus.
- Father, by Your mighty hand upon my life, I receive the power from on high to be steps ahead of my enemies, in the mighty name of Jesus.
- Father, let every activity of evil powers fashioned against the fulfillment of my destiny and happiness be put to open shame and be frustrated, in the name of Jesus.
- Father, by your mighty power I command every barrier placed on my journey to the

realization of my purpose in life and destiny be lifted, in the name of Jesus.

- Father, just as it is written that strangers will flee from their closed places, therefore, I command every hiding enemy plotting setbacks against my progress to be exposed by the light of God and be silenced by the blood of Jesus, in the mighty name of Jesus.

- Father, by the authority of Christ in me, I bind the power that has been assigned to make life difficult for me, in the name of Jesus.

- Father, by Your mighty power, I take authority over forces of darkness militating against my glory and blessings and have made God look like a liar.

- I decree that they be cast into the bottomless pit, in the name of Jesus.

- Father, cause confusion in the camp of my adversaries and let all their evil counsel against me and my family come to naught, in the mighty name of Jesus.

- Father, I decree the expiration of the activities of any devil oppressing my handwork, in the name of Jesus.
- Father, by the authority given to me, I command Satan to take its hands off of my life and destiny, in the mighty name of Jesus.
- Father, I'm glad because I know my battle is the Lord's and He is my shield. Therefore, I dwell in God's secret place, fearing no evil, and I cause the wrath of God to fall on my enemies, in the mighty name of Jesus.
- Father, by the authority in your Word, I put an end to every attack of the devil and his cohorts in my life and destiny, in the mighty name of Jesus.
- Father, the Lord is my shepherd, and I shall not want, The enemy may try, but God has the final say over my life and my destiny, in the mighty name of Jesus. Psalm 44:4: "Thou art my King, O God: command deliverances for Jacob."

- Father, fight for me and command deliverance for me from strong powers, in the name of Jesus.
- Father, Let the fire of God consume every dark scheme against me and confuse every gathering where conspiracy is being made concerning me, in the mighty name of Jesus. Psalm 2:4: "He that sitteth in the heavens shall laugh: the Lord shall have them in derision."
- Let God laugh the laugh of victory over every opposition in my life, in the name of Jesus.
- Psalm 11:5: "The righteousness of the perfect shall direct his way: but the wicked shall fall by his wickedness." I am the righteousness of God in Christ, bringing God's kingdom to earth.
- I stand against every form of wickedness in my life and environment, and I decree the fall of every devil and his cohorts, in the mighty name of Jesus.
- Isaiah 8:10: "Take counsel together, and it shall come to naught; speak the word, and it shall

not stand for God is with us." God is with me always, therefore, evil counsels are brought to waste, in the name of Jesus.

- Proverbs 26:27a: "Whoso diggeth a pit shall fall therein." I shall not fall into any trap, and just as it is written, the trap shall get its owner, in the mighty name of Jesus.

- Psalm 7:6a: "Arise, O Lord, in Your anger; Lift Yourself up because of the rage of my enemies." Let the devil that is determined to destroy me, destroy himself, by the power in the name of Jesus.

- 2 Samuel 15:31b: "And David said, 'O Lord, I pray, turn the counsel of Ahithophel into foolishness!" O Lord, turn the wisdom of my enemies to foolishness and let shame be their portion, in the mighty name of Jesus.

- Psalm 27:2: "When the wicked, even mine enemies and my foes, came upon me to eat up my flesh, they stumbled and fell."

- Father, let every flesh-eating and blood-sucking adversary in my life and destiny fall and die, in the mighty name of Jesus.

- Revelation 12:11a: "And they overcame him by the blood of the Lamb." By the blood of Jesus, I overcame every demonic force chasing helpers away from my life and my destiny, in the name of Jesus.

- Colossians 2:15: "...and having spoiled principalities and powers, he made a shew of them openly, triumphing over them in it." Father, put to shame every power of darkness lying in wait to destroy your calling and purpose upon my life, in the mighty name of Jesus.

- Psalm 58:6: "Break their teeth, O God, in their mouth: break out the great teeth of the young lions, O Lord." Father, rebuke the devil and his agents and disarm them for my sake, in the mighty name of Jesus.

- Psalm 35:3: "Draw out also the spear and stop the way against them that persecute me: say unto my soul, I am thy salvation." You are my salvation Lord and my help. Father, draw out your spear and wield it against my persecutors and let them flee from my life and destiny, in the mighty name of Jesus.

- Psalm 119:134: "Deliver me from the oppression of man: so I will keep thy precepts." Abba Father, deliver my soul from the devil and those who seek after it to destroy it and give me victory over them, in the mighty name of Jesus.

- The battle is of the Lord's, and this fills me with confidence. Disgrace the enemy, oh Lord, and cause every mountain in my life to melt away.

- I declare that I abide under the protection of Christ. I am immune from the weapons and accusations of my enemies, who seek my destruction. I cast every spirit warring against me into bondage. I declare myself victorious in Jesus' name.

- Lord, I cry unto you this evil day. Hear my cry, O Lord, and save me by your grace from trouble.
- I exercise my God-given dominion over my environment and my territories.
- I am unlimited and I rise above every demonic standard.
- God in me is far greater than he that is in the world, so I declare that no devil or spirit can conquer me.
- Every altar that has been raised to limit my lineage is destroyed in the name of Jesus. Let the judgment of the Lord come upon every generational enemy and pattern in my family in Jesus' name.
- Oh Lord, I declare that every enemy assigned to hinder me from progressing or positioned to truncate my success shall die by fire. Let the fire of God come against every demon that wants to rip my success from me, in Jesus' name.
- Every power that wants to make me fail and cause my destiny to become useless, let thunder

from heaven strike you in the name of Jesus. Let every man or woman that will separate me from my destiny be divinely separated from me in Jesus' name.

- Lord, I come against all my enemies. Cause your angels to arise and wage war on my behalf, in Jesus' name.

- Every enemy that has refused to let me live in peace, become troubled, in

  Jesus' name. Let the light of the Lord destroy them. I am free in Jesus' name

- O Lord, let there be casualties against all the demonic powers operating in my neighborhood and family lineage in Jesus' name.

- Let a destructive storm from heaven come against every demonic plan that is plotted against me and my family in Jesus' name.

- Oh Mighty God, let there be shaking and scattering in the camp of the enemy, in the mighty name of Jesus.

- Lord God, let every evil transaction against my progress scatter by fire, in Jesus' name.
- Lord, let your wrath fall mightily upon my enemies and let no one escape from your destructive power, in Jesus' name.
- O Lord, let every tongue professing evil upon my life and destiny be cut off, in Jesus' name.
- Lord, cause everlasting trouble to come upon those that trouble me. Let them and their generation be troubled forever, in Jesus' name.
- Dear God, cause the eye of every monitoring spirit and agent of my family to be blinded in the name of Jesus.
- Let every evil arrow shot against my family backfire to the ravaging of its senders, in Jesus' name.
- Lord, cause my head to be lifted far above the plots and plans of my enemies, in Jesus' name.
- Father Lord, I tread on serpents, scorpions, and over every power of the enemy. Nothing shall hurt me in Jesus' name.

- By the Word of God, I declare that I am more than a conqueror and I conquer all my enemies, in Jesus' name.

- Father, condemn every tongue and evil speaking made against me and my family, in Jesus' name.

- O Lord, cause any enemy that has risen to thwart me, be woefully thwarted in my stead, in Jesus' name, Amen.

- As the mountains surround Jerusalem, so the Lord surrounds His people from this time forth and forever. For the scepter of wickedness shall not rest on the land allotted to the righteous, Lest the righteous reach out their hands to iniquity. (Psalm 125: 1-2)

- God judgeth the righteous, and God is angry with the wicked every day.

 (Psalms 7:11)

- Thou art my hiding place; thou shall preserve me from trouble; thou shall encompass me with songs of deliverance. (Psalm 32:7)

- Except the Lord built the house, they labor in vain that built it: except the Lord keeps the city, the watchman waketh but in vain. (Psalm 127: 1)
- Though I walk in the midst of trouble, thou will revive me. Thou will stretch forth thy hand against the wrath of my enemies, and thy right hand shall save me. (Psalm 138:7)
- For thou hast delivered my soul from death. Wilt thou not deliver my feet from falling that I may walk before God in the light of the living? (Psalm 56:13)
- The Lord is my rock and my fortress and my deliverer; my God, my strength, in whom will I trust; my buckler and the horn of my salvation, and my high tower. (Psalm 18:2)
- Let Holy Ghost Fire destroy every hidden disease or infirmity seeking to operate in my body, in the name of Jesus.
- My Lord, protect me from any sickness in my life. Shield me under your wings, in Jesus' name.

- It's by your mercy, Lord, that I am protected from sicknesses and diseases. Let your angels continue to safeguard me, in Jesus' name.
- Lord, remove from my body every form of illness. Give strength to my bones and renew my health, in Jesus' name.
- Lord, your might cannot be quantified. You have protected me since my youth. Help me not to take your protection for granted, in Jesus' name.
- O Lord, continue to preserve my body from ill-health. Help me to spend time on the activities that will improve the quality of my health, in Jesus' name.
- I come against any type of sickness in my body. My body is the temple of God so sickness is an outcast. Get out of my body, in Jesus' name.
- I declare that every part of my body shall continue to perform in optimal health, in Jesus' name.

- I declare that I am protected from every devilish counsel that wants me to die prematurely, in Jesus' name.
- Let every satanic dart thrown against my health return to its sender immediately, in Jesus' name.
- Every satanic agent monitoring my health, I come against you by the fire of the Holy Ghost, in Jesus' name.
- declare that the shield of the Lord is upon me, covering me from every Satanic manipulation against enjoying sound health, in Jesus' name.
- Holy Ghost fire, destroy every satanic seed of illness in my blood, flesh and bone, in Jesus' name.
- Let every altar attempting to project sicknesses and diseases upon my family be destroyed, in the name of Jesus.
- O Lord, cause hell and its agents to release their hold over my health, in Jesus' name.

- I decree that I am renewed and preserved in my health and in my mind, in Jesus' name.
- Lord, build a hedge of protection around me and my household. Cause your protection to cover every aspect of my life and my family, in Jesus' name.
- Dear Lord, you are my defender. You are the fortress I hide in. Let me not be snatched from your hand. Defend me from the enemy's plans.
- Preserve me and my family, oh Lord. Preserve me from the arrow that flies by day, the destruction that wastes at noonday, and the pestilence that walks in darkness, in Jesus' name.
- Though my enemies attack in their hundreds and thousands, I declare by the Word of God that none shall come near me.
- O Lord, keep me from those who see evil as good and good as evil. Let the schemes of the unrighteous fail, in Jesus' name.
- Father Lord, strengthen me to cast down every evil thought and imagination that the devil is

trying to plant in my mind to make me susceptible to him, in Jesus' name.

- Father Lord, send your angels to cover me and my household. Send them to fight every evil that I cannot see, in Jesus' name.

- I look up to you as my Protector. Help me to align myself with you at all times and stay under the umbrella of your protection, in Jesus' name.

- Lord, I commit myself and my family into your hands, as we battle each day against sin, Satan and sickness; preserve us in these battles, in Jesus' name.

- Lord, I exist for your purpose. Preserve my health so that the purpose you created me for will be fulfilled.

- Lord Jesus, protect me from every thought and idea that will draw me from you. Rather let your Word come alive in my heart.

- Lord, destroy self in me. Protect me from the influence of self and help me to remember you are the owner of my life.

- I wear the armor of God, and with it, I come against the wiles of the enemy, in Jesus' name.
- I pray that every pattern of accidents that cause untimely death in my family be destroyed, in Jesus' name.
- Lord, cause wailing and tears to go far away from me and my family, in Jesus' name.
- Lord, let your innumerable company of angels follow me to all places, in Jesus' name.
- Any satanic plan to stop my destiny from manifesting through accidents fails by fire, in Jesus' name.
- Every accident that has been staged against me and my family, I come against you in the name of Jesus. I redeem my days, weeks, months, and years. I sabotage every accident whether on land, water, or air, in Jesus' name.
- In Jesus' name, let every grave that has been planted on land, sea, or air for me or my family be destroyed by the blood of the Lamb.

- As I walk through the valley of the shadow of death, Lord, help me to remember that you are with me so I will not fear any evil, in Jesus' name.
- As I go to work, go before me Lord, and cause any exalted place to be leveled in my life, in Jesus' name.
- Lord, let every mountain or valley of accident that has been planted before me be destroyed, in Jesus' name.
- Lord, uproot any planted tree that is not of you in my life. Let any accident staged by the devil over my family be cut off by your wrath, in Jesus' name.
- I declare that I am anointed by the blood of Jesus, so when I am faced with an accident, it shall pass over me, in Jesus' name.
- It is written that I shall not die but live and declare the works of the Lord in the land of the living. So any devilish plot to kill me and my

household be destroyed out of our lives, in Jesus' name.

- God's thoughts for me are good and not evil to give me an expected end. So I know that accidents are not my expected end. I come against any plan that is not of Christ for my life, in Jesus' name.

- Lord do not hold your peace concerning me. Let the roads I will take be anointed by Christ's blood, in Jesus' Name.

- I come against every power plotting accidents and disasters for my family be consumed by the fire of the Holy Ghost, in Jesus' name.

- It is written that I will go out with joy and return with peace, I declare that as I go out, I will be enveloped in the joy of Christ and return in His peace, in Jesus' name.

Notes

Notes

Intentionally Left Blank